21st Century
Basic Skills
Library

KITTENS GROW UP TO BE CATS

by Cecilia Minden, PhD

Cherry Lake Publishing • Ann Arbor, Michigan

1

Published in the United States of America
by Cherry Lake Publishing
Ann Arbor, Michigan
www.cherrylakepublishing.com

Photo Credits: Cover and page 1, ©Artsiom Kireyau/Shutterstock, Inc.;
page 4, ©Aldo Danti/Shutterstock, Inc.; page 6, ©iStockphoto.com/
Claudiad; page 8, ©Lindsay Dean/Shutterstock, Inc.; page 10, ©Igor
Sokolov (breeze)/Shutterstock, Inc.; page 12, ©Petspicture/Shutterstock,
Inc.; page 14, ©Maszas/Dreamstime.com; page 16, ©Natalya
Kudritskaya/Shutterstock, Inc.; page 18, ©Tony Campbell/Shutterstock,
Inc.; page 20, ©Itayuri/Dreamstime.com

Library of Congress Cataloging-in-Publication Data
Minden, Cecilia.
  Kittens grow up to be cats/by Cecilia Minden.
     p. cm.—(21st century basic skills library. Level 1)
  Includes bibliographical references and index.
  ISBN-13: 978-1-60279-852-6 (lib. bdg.)
  ISBN-10: 1-60279-852-4 (lib. bdg.)
  1. Kittens—Juvenile literature. I. Title. II. Series.
  SF445.7.M56 2010
  636.8'07—dc22   2009048595

Cherry Lake Publishing would like to acknowledge
the work of The Partnership for 21st Century Skills.
Please visit *www.21stcenturyskills.org* for more information.

Printed in the United States of America
Corporate Graphics Inc.
July 2010
CLFA07

TABLE OF CONTENTS

Kittens

This tiny **bundle** of fur is a baby cat.

Baby cats are called kittens.

They cannot see or hear.

They like to nap.

A **queen** is a mama cat.

She keeps her kittens safe and warm.

Growing Up

Soon the kittens can smell and hear.

Kittens can see when they are 2 weeks old.

Kittens get **teeth** when they are 1 month old.

Kittens like to run.

They will play with other kittens.

Cats

A kitten is an **adult** cat when it is 1 year old.

Then it can have kittens of its own!

Find Out More

BOOK

Van Fleet, Matthew, and Brian Stanton (photographer). *Cats.*
New York: Simon & Schuster Books for Young Readers, 2009.

WEB SITE

CFA For Kids—About Cats: Feline Education for Youngsters
kids.cfa.org
Find cat information, games, and pictures.

Glossary

adult (UH-dult) an animal that has reached its full size and can have its own babies

bundle (BUN-duhl) a group of things fastened together

queen (KWEEN) an adult female cat

teeth (TEETH) white, bony objects in an animal's mouth that help it bite and chew

Home and School Connection

Use this list of words from the book to help your child become a better reader. Word games and writing activities can help beginning readers reinforce literacy skills.

a	growing	of	the
adult	have	old	then
an	hear	or	they
and	her	other	this
are	is	own	tiny
baby	it	play	to
bundle	its	queen	up
called	keeps	run	warm
can	kitten	safe	weeks
cannot	kittens	see	when
cat	like	she	will
cats	mama	smell	with
fur	month	soon	year
get	nap	teeth	

Index

About the Author

Cecilia Minden is the former Director of the Language and Literacy Program at the Harvard Graduate School of Education. She currently works as a literacy consultant for school and library publishers and is the author of more than 100 books for children.